Camille Saint-Saëns
(1835–1921)

Karneval der Tiere
Große zoologische Phantasie

Für Klavier leicht bearbeitet von
Hans-Günter Heumann

Zeichnungen von Brigitte Smith

The Carnival of the Animals
A great zoological fantasy

In a simple arrangement for piano
by Hans-Günter Heumann

Drawings by Brigitte Smith

ED 23570
ISMN 979-0-001-21570-1
ISBN 978-3-7957-2571-6

SCHOTT

Mainz · London · Madrid · Paris · New York · Tokyo · Beijing
© 1992/2022 Schott Music GmbH & Co. KG, Mainz · Printed in Germany
www.schott-music.com

Liebe Klavierspielerin,
lieber Klavierspieler,

in diesem Band wird das großartige Werk *Karneval der Tiere* von Camille Saint-Saëns (1835–1921) in leichter Bearbeitung für Klavier vorgestellt.

Dargestellt in einer „großen zoologischen Phantasie" treffen sich Tiere zu einer lustigen Karnevalsparty.

Dem Komponisten Saint-Saëns gelang es, durch die verschiedenen Orchesterinstrumente und selbstverständlich durch seine packende Musik die Tiere so genau darzustellen, dass man sie deutlich hören kann, so z. B. das Gebrüll des Löwen, das Gegacker der Hühner, die schweren Schritte des Elefanten, das Hüpfen der Känguruhs.

So, nun auf zum *Karneval der Tiere*, und viel Spaß beim Spielen!

Euer
Hans-Günter Heumann

Dear Pianists,

In this volume you will find a simple arrangement for piano of *The Carnival of the Animals*, a wonderful composition by Camille Saint-Saëns (1835–1921).

As they are presented in this 'great zoological fantasy', we hear the animals getting together to celebrate a carnival party.

With stirring tunes, and by drawing on the sounds of the various instruments of the orchestra, Saint-Saëns managed to portray the animals in such detail that you can hear them quite clearly: the roar of the lion, the cackling of the hens, the heavy steps of the elephant and the jumping of the kangaroos.

Now, off you go to *The Carnival of the Animals* – have fun playing your way through the story!

With best wishes,
Hans-Günter Heumann

Inhalt

Contents

Steckbrief
Karneval der Tiere

Komponiert Februar 1886 in Wien

Uraufführung 9. März 1886 in einem Hauskonzert (keine weitere Aufführung)

Originaltitel auf französisch: LE CARNAVAL DES ANIMAUX

Orchesterbesetzung 2 Klaviere, Flöte, Klarinette, 2 Violinen, Viola, Violoncello, Kontrabass, Xylophon, Harmonium

Veröffentlichung des Werkes nach dem Tode des Komponisten im Jahre 1922

History of the Work
The Carnival of the Animals

Composed in Vienna, February 1886

First performed on 9 March 1886 in a private concert (no other performances followed)

Original title in French LE CARNAVAL DES ANIMAUX

Orchestral scoring 2 pianos, flute, clarinet, 2 violins, viola, cello, double bass, xylophone, harmonium

Published in 1922, after the death of the composer

Steckbrief
Camille Saint-Saëns

1835 geboren am 9. Oktober in Paris

1840 Beginn des Klavierunterrichts

1841 erste Kompositionen

1846 erstes öffentliches Konzert

1848 Eintritt in das Pariser Konservatorium (studierte Orgel und Komposition)

ab 1853 Organist an verschiedenen Kirchen in Paris (bis 1877)

1861 Lehrauftrag an der Niedermeyerschule

ab 1877 ohne Amt tätig. Konzertreisen als Dirigent und Pianist (vorwiegend mit eigenen Werken)

1921 stirbt am 16. Dezember in Algier

Biography
Camille Saint-Saëns

1835 born in Paris on 9 October

1840 started piano lessons

1841 composed his first pieces of music

1846 gave his first public concert performance

1848 entered the Paris Conservatoire (studied organ and composition)

from 1853 organist at various churches in Paris (until 1877)

1861 teaching post at Niedermeyer school

from 1877 freelance musician. Concert tours as conductor and pianist (chiefly in performances of his own works)

1921 died in Algiers on 16 December

Königlicher Marsch des Löwen
The Royal March of the Lion

Allegro non troppo ♩ = 88

Più allegro ♩ = 176

Hühner und Hähne
Hens and Cocks

Allegro moderato ♩ = 116

Hemione

Wilde Esel || Wild Asses

Presto furioso ♩ = 120

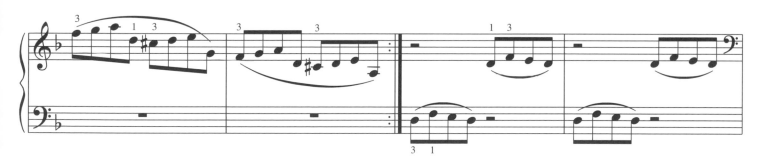

Schildkröten
Turtles

Andante maestoso ♪ = 80

* Motiv (Cancan) aus der Operette „Orpheus in der Unterwelt" von Jacques Offenbach / Motif (Cancan) from the operetta 'Orpheus in the Underworld' by Jacques Offenbach

Der Elefant
The Elephant

Allegretto pomposo ♩ = 120

* Motiv (Sylphentanz) aus der dramatischen Legende „Fausts Verdammung" von Hector Berlioz / Motif (Dance of the Sylphs) from the dramatic legend 'The Damnation of Faust' by Hector Berlioz

Känguruhs
Kangaroos

Aquarium
The Aquarium

Persönlichkeiten mit langen Ohren
Characters With Long Ears

Tempo ad lib. ($\bullet$ = 100)

* Vor jedem Ton „e" in der rechten Hand kann ad libitum eine kurze Vorschlagsnote „dis" gespielt werden. / A short grace note (D♯) may be played ad libitum before the E in the right hand.

Der Kuckuck im tiefen Wald
The Cuckoo Deep in the Wood

Das Vogelhaus
The Aviary

Pianisten*
The Pianists*

Allegro moderato ♩ = 132

* Nach Ansicht von Saint-Saëns gehören die Pianisten mit ihren endlosen, langweiligen Tonleitern und ihrem tierischen Ernst auch schon fast zur Tierwelt. / In the opinion of Saint-Saëns, pianists are a strange, almost animal-like species, playing endless, boring scales with the utmost seriousness.

Fossilien
The Fossils

Allegro ridicolo $\dot{=} = 88$

Der Schwan*
The Swan*

* Dieses wohl bekannteste Musikstück aus diesem Zyklus wurde von der berühmten Tänzerin Anna Pawlowa als „sterbender Schwan" unvergesslich getanzt. / This most well-known piece from the cycle was danced unforgettably by the famous ballerina Anna Pavlova as the 'dying swan'.

Finale

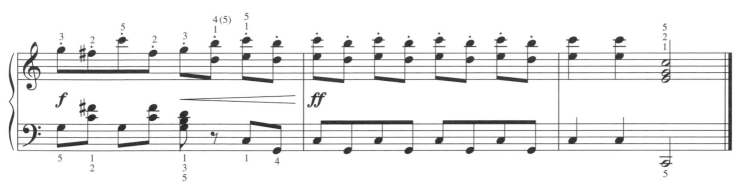

Schott Music, Mainz 60 114

Fantasievolle Klaviermusik / Imaginative Piano Music

Themenhefte in der Reihe „Schott Piano Classics"
Collections on various topics in the 'Schott Piano Classics' series
Herausgegeben von / Edited by Monika Twelsiek

- Unbekanntes entdecken
- Bekanntes in neuem Licht sehen
- Spannende und vielfarbige Themenhefte
- für den anspruchsvollen Unterricht
- leicht bis mittelschwer

- discover unfamiliar pieces
- see familiar pieces in a new light
- stimulating and colourful thematic collections
- for interesting and challenging tuition
- easy to intermediate level

Impressionismus / Impressionism

27 Originalwerke rund um Debussy – zum Eintauchen in die schwerelose Welt des Impressionismus

27 original pieces, grouped around Debussy – for immersion in the weightless world of impressionism
ED 9042

Programmmusik / Programme Music

40 Originalwerke, die mit programmatischen Titeln die Fantasie anregen – „Im Wald", „Regen", „Mondschein", „Sport", „Technik" u.a.

40 original pieces with programmatic titles stimulating the imagination – 'In the Forest', 'Rain', 'Moonlight', 'Sport', 'Technology' etc.
ED 9043

Reisebilder / Travel Pictures

37 Originalwerke zum Erkunden fremder Welten, – musikalische Ansichtskarten einer Reise in die unterschiedlichsten Länder

37 original pieces exploring foreign lands – musical postcards illustrate a journey in the most various countries
ED 9044

Emotionen / Emotions

35 Originalwerke zum Lachen und Weinen – schillernde Gefühle, die durch Musik erweckt und dargestellt werden

35 original pieces to inspire laughter and tears – dazzling feelings that are described and evoked by music
ED 9045

Walzer / Waltzes

48 Originalwerke von Mozart bis Ligeti – Walzer für jeden Tag: derb und übermütig, verträumt und melancholisch, langsam und virtuos

48 original pieces ranging from Mozart to Ligeti – waltzes for every day of the week: robust and exuberant, dreamy and melancholy, slow and elaborate
ED 9047

Nacht und Träume / Night and Dreams

36 Originalwerke zum Chillen, Relaxen, Entspannen – zum Eintauchen in die „Blaue Stunde", zum Tag- und Nacht-Träumen

36 original pieces for chilling out, relaxing, unwinding – for dipping into the twilight mood of dreams and daydreams
ED 9048

Tempo! Tempo!

40 schnelle und wilde, furiose und virtuose, rasante und riskante, billante und fulminante Originalwerke von Barock bis Rock – ein Etüdenheft der besonderen Art!

40 fast and furious, rousing and masterly, dazzling and brilliant original pieces ranging from Baroque to Rock, in a highly unusual book of studies!
ED 9049

Spielsachen / Toys

44 leichte Originalwerke für Kinder und Erwachsene – von Puppen, Teddybären, Spieluhren und Computerspielen zum Spielen und Erinnern

44 easy original pieces for children and adults to play, bringing back memories of dolls, teddy bears, musical boxes and computer games
ED 9055

Wasser / Water

25 Originalwerke zum Eintauchen in Quellen, Bäche, Flüsse, Meere – Wasser hat einen Klang und einen Rhythmus, es fließt – wie die Musik

25 original pieces plunge into springs, streams, rivers and seas – water has a sound and a rhythm, it flows – like music
ED 22276

Präludien / Preludes

40 Originalwerke aus fünf Jahrhunderten von Johann Sebastian Bach bis Nikolai Kapustin – eine klingende Geschichte der Gattung "Präludium"

40 original works ranging across five Centuries, from Johann Sebastian Bach to Nikolai Kapustin – a musical history of the Prelude
ED 23405

SCHOTT
www.schott-music.com